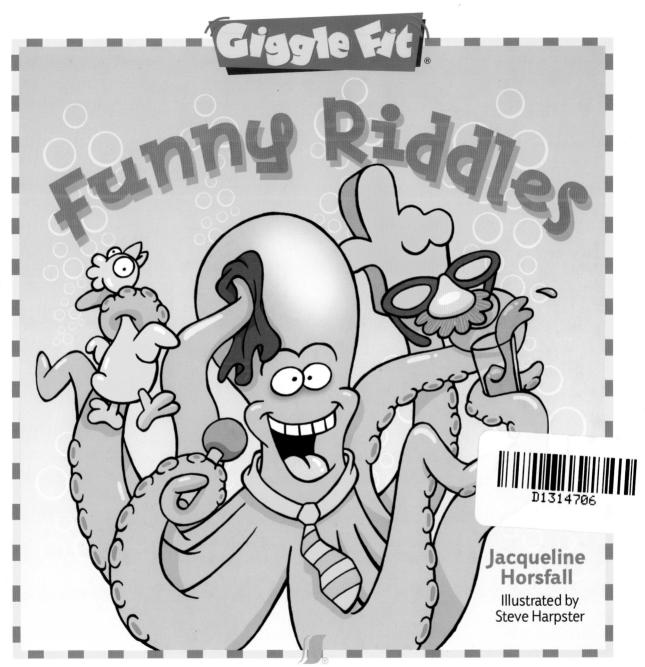

Giggle Fit

Funny Riddles

Jacqueline
Horsfall

Illustrated by
Steve Harpster

Sterling Publishing Co., Inc. New York

Library of Congress Cataloging-in-Publication Data available

10   9   8   7   6   5   4   3   2   1

Published in paperback in 2006 by Sterling Publishing Co., Inc.
387 Park Avenue South, New York, NY 10016
© 2003 by Jacqueline Horsfall
Distributed in Canada by Sterling Publishing,
c/o Canadian Manda Group, 165 Dufferin Street,
Toronto, Ontario, Canada M6K 3H6
Distributed in the United Kingdom by GMC Distribution Services,
Castle Place, 166 High Street, Lewes, East Sussex, England BN7 1XU
Distributed in Australia by Capricorn Link (Australia) Pty. Ltd.,
P.O. Box 704, Windsor, NSW 2756, Australia

Printed in China

Sterling   ISBN-13:   978-1-4027-0864-0   Hardcover
       ISBN-10:   1-4027-0864-5

       ISBN-13:   978-1-4027-2770-2   Paperback
       ISBN-10:   1-4027-2770-4

For information about custom editions, special sales, premium and
corporate purchases, please contact Sterling Special Sales
Department at 800-805-5489 or specialsales@sterlingpub.com.

What has teeth but can't bite?
A comb.

What has hands, but never washes them?
A clock.

What always disappears when you stand up?
Your lap.

What do you get when you cross your right eye with your left eye?
Dizzy.

What time does a doctor
get up?
Sicks o'clock.

What time does a tennis
player get up?
Ten—ish.

What time does a shark get up?
Ate o'clock.

What time does a
duck get up?
**At the quack of
dawn.**

What has 88 keys, but never opens a door?
A piano.

Why do vampires brush their teeth?
So they won't have bat breath.

Who taught King Tut to brush his teeth?
His mummy.

What happened to the skunk that fell into the bathtub?
It stunk all the way to the bottom.

What do you call a little bear who never takes a bath?
Winnie the Phew!

What happened to the mouse that fell into the bathtub?
It came out squeaky clean.

What should you do if you find a great white shark in your bathtub?
Pull out the plug!

How does a bear test its bath water?
With its bear feet.

What do you take when you bring a cell phone into the bathtub with you?
A babble bath.

Why can't elephants ever really get clean?
Because they can't take off their trunks.

Why did the rabbit wear a shower cap?
It didn't want to get its hare wet.

How can you be sure to keep your hair dry in the shower?
Don't turn on the water.

Why did the basketball players shower after every game?
Because they dribble all over the place.

If you held six bars of soap in one hand and 10 in the other, what would you have?
Very big hands!

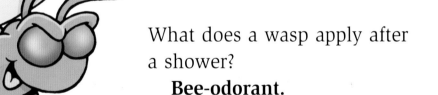

What does a wasp apply after a shower?
Bee-odorant.

What do cheerleaders eat
for breakfast?
Cheer-ee-ohs!

What do cats eat
for breakfast?
Mice Krispies.

What do race car drivers eat
for breakfast?
Fast food.

What does a basketball team
do for breakfast?
Dunk donuts.

What do dogs eat
for breakfast?
Pooched eggs.

What do canaries
eat for breakfast?
Cream of Tweet.

What does Humpty
Dumpty eat for breakfast?
Egg drop soup.

Why was the broom late for school?
It overswept.

Why was Silly Billy afraid to go to school?
He had class-trophobia.

What is the first thing a dolphin learns in class?
Its A-B-Seas.

Why do dolphins swim in salt water?
Pepper makes them sneeze.

How do dogs do in school?
They have a ruff time.

Why was the polar bear
upset with her test grade?
It was 20 below zero.

How did the lettuce get an
A on the test?
It used its head.

What should you do if you get a B on
your math test?
Be careful it doesn't sting you.

What did the ocean say to the oyster?
"What time do you open up?"

How does Neptune keep his underwater castle clean?
He hires mer-maids.

What did the ocean say to the pier?
"There's something fishy going on here."

What do bumblebees wear on the beach?
Bee-kinis.

How do spiders
swim laps?
They do the crawl.

How do caterpillars
swim laps?
They do the butterfly.

How do chickens
swim laps?
**They do the
breaststroke.**

How do vets
swim laps?
**They do the dog
paddle.**

How does the Man in the Moon eat soup?
With a Big Dipper.

What is the messiest constellation?
The Big Dripper.

What Olympic high jumper can jump higher than the moon?
All of them. The moon can't jump.

How would you phone the Man in the Moon?
Use E.T.& T.

How do you get a baby astronaut to go to sleep?
You rock-et.

How do you know that Saturn has taken a bath in your tub?
It leaves a ring.

17

What do you have when your head is hot, your foot is cold, and you see spots before your eyes?
A polka-dot sock over your head.

When can a horse leave the hospital and go home?
When it's in stable condition.

What do you do with a squeaky mouse?
Oil it.

Where do sick frogs go?
To the hopsital.

Where do ships go when
they get seasick?
To the dock-tor.

If you try to cross the ocean in a leaky ship,
what do you get?
About halfway.

What's the fastest way to get to the hospital?
Pick a fight with a dinosaur.

What happened when the owl got a sore throat?
It didn't give a hoot.

What television programs do cows watch?
Mooo-vies.

What television sets do zebras watch?
Black and white ones.

What television programs do slugs watch?
Slime-time dramas.

When you go to the movies, do you need supervision?

No, regular vision will do.

Why couldn't Ms. Skunk get into the movie theater?

She was ten scents short.

What did the famous movie star dog do after its performance?

Took a bow-wow.

What runs around all day and then lies under the bed with its tongue hanging out?
Your sneaker.

What do video cassettes do at night?
They unwind.

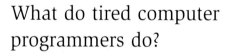

What do tired computer programmers do?
They go home and crash.

Why can't computers remember their dreams?
Because they are always losing their memories.

How do insects communicate
on their computers?
By bee-mail.

What happened to the
computer programmer's
cheese sandwich?
His mouse ate it.

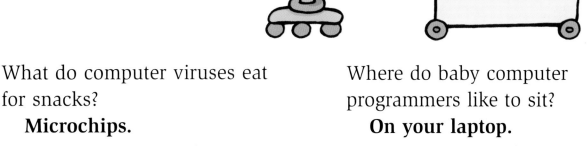

What do computer viruses eat
for snacks?
Microchips.

Where do baby computer
programmers like to sit?
On your laptop.

Why did Dracula's computer die?
He took a few bytes out of it.

What did the pen say
to the pencil?
"So what's your point?"

Why should you take a
pen to the garden?
**So you can weed
and write.**

What's the only word in
the dictionary always
pronounced incorrectly?
Incorrectly.

Is it bad to write on an
empty stomach?
**No, but it's better to write
on paper.**

What kind of ship can last forever?
Friend-ship.

What keys won't fit in any door?
The Florida Keys.

What speaks every language?
An echo.

Why is the letter "t" like an island?
It's in the middle of water.

How do pigs communicate?
In swine language.

What vegetable do you get when a dinosaur tromps through your garden?
Squash.

What does Santa do in his garden?
Hoe-hoe-hoe.

What do vegetables give each other when they get married?
Onion rings.

What vegetable do chickens grow in their gardens?
Eggplant.

Why couldn't the Cow Who Jumped Over the Moon eat her potato salad?
The dish ran away with the spoon.

Why did the truck driver stop on the highway to eat his spaghetti?
He saw a fork in the road.

What should you do if you don't like Swiss cheese on your burger?
Just eat the holes and leave the Swiss cheese on your plate.

Why did the belt get arrested?
It held up a pair of pants.

What kind of ape lives in a gym?
A gympanzee.

Why can't centipedes skateboard?
They can't afford 100 knee pads.

What do you get when you cross a kangaroo with a snake ?
A jump rope.

What kind of bikes do polar bears ride?
Ice-cycles.

What did the glove say to the baseball?

"Catch you later!"

Where does the catcher sit at the dinner table?

Behind the plate.

Why does a pitcher raise one leg when he pitches?

If he raises both, he falls down.

Why are spiders good baseball players?

They catch lots of flies.

Why do fish go after worms?
Because they're hooked on them.

What's the best way to communicate with a trout?
Drop it a line.

Why didn't Noah do too much fishing on the Ark?
He only had two worms.

Why can't Batman and Robin go fishing?
Robin eats all the worms.

Where do chickens
get off the highway?
At the eggs-it.

Where do old bicycle tires go?
To the old spokes home.

Why did the bubblegum
cross the road?
**It was stuck on the
chicken's foot.**

Why do birds fly south
for the winter?
**Because they can't
afford a cruise.**

What do you say to a skeleton
going on a cruise?
Bone Voyage!

Why can't you play cards on a cruise?
**Because the passengers sit on all
the decks.**

What does the Sandman
pack his clothes in?
A nap-sack.

What do parachute
jumpers pack their
gear in?
Air bags.

What do boxers pack
their clothes in?
Sluggage.

What kind of uniforms do
paratroopers wear?
Jump suits.

Why did the bus driver go broke?
He drove all his customers away.

How can you tell if a train has just gone by?
You can see its tracks.

What does a dragon do when he misses the train?
Dragon fly.

What happened when
dinosaurs started driving?
**They had tyrannosaurus
wrecks.**

What do clowns do when
they get into a car?
Chuckle-up.

Why was the tow truck
on the speedway?
**It was trying to pull
a fast one.**

What kind of car starts with T?
Cars don't start with tea, they start with gas.

Why can't you take a turkey out for dinner?
Because he gobbles his food.

What do gophers do when they're hungry?
Gopher a pizza.

What did the duck say when it was finished eating?
"Put it on my bill."

What should you do if there's onion soup on the menu?
Wipe it off.

Why was the giraffe so late for the party?

Its mother told it to wash its neck.

Why was the rabbit so late for the party?

It had to go to the hare-dresser.

Why was E.T. so late for the party?

He had to phone home.

Why are horses terrible dancers?
They have two left feet.

How do baby chicks dance?
Cheep-to-cheep.

What kind of dancing do owls do?
The whoo-la.

Who should you call if you want to square dance on the beach?
The fiddler crab.

What did the goblins sing at the party?
Rhythm and boos.

What did the bumblebees
sing at the party?
BeeBop.

What did the mummy
sing at the party?
Wrap.

What did the computer programmer
sing at the party?
Disc-o.

What did Bigfoot say when he stepped on your foot?
"I've got a crush on you."

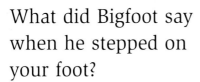

What did the moose do in front of the mirror?
Flex his mooscles.

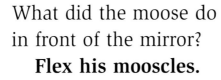

When the two snakes got married, what did their towels say?
Hiss and Hers.

Who is beautiful, gray, and wore big slippers to the ball?
Cinderelephant.

What does Cinderella wear at the beach?
Glass flippers.

Where did Cinderella Spaghetti dream she was going?
To the Meat Ball.

Who invented spaghetti?
Someone who used his noodle.

What's the difference between a football player and a duck?
One's in a huddle, the other's in a puddle.

Why do elephants have tusks?
They can't afford braces.

What would you get if you crossed a sheep and a monkey?
A baaa-boon.

Who stays with young squids when their parents go out?
Baby-squidders.

How do you get rid of bedbugs?
Make them sleep on the sofa.

What happened to the Boy Scout who bought a camouflage sleeping bag?
He couldn't find it.

What animal pouts when it has to go to bed?
A whine-ocerous.

Why do you have to go to bed?
Because the bed won't come to you.

What has a waterbed
but never rests?
A river.

What is a billow?
**What you sleep on when
you have a bad cold.**

What is the difference between a baker
and an elephant?
One bakes the bread, the other breaks the bed.

What would you do if you trapped an elephant in your pajamas?
Make him take them off.

Why did Silly Billy wear Zorro's cape to bed?
So he could catch some Z's.

Why is it good to have holes in your underwear?
So you can put your legs through.

What do lawyers wear
to bed?

Their briefs.

What did King Arthur wear
to bed?

His knight-y.

What does a slice of toast wear
to bed?

Jam-mies.

Why did Silly Sarah keep an exercise bike in her bedroom?

She was tired of walking in her sleep.

When do you stop at green and go at red?

When you're eating a watermelon.

What does Mama Snake give her babies before they go to sleep?

Hugs and hisses.

What toys do baby snakes take to bed?

Their rattles.

INDEX